I Can Get Ready For School

Written by Chemise Taylor

Illustrated by Alexis B. Taylor

Copyright © 2019 by My Skills Books

Published by My Skills Books

All rights reserved. No part of this publication may be reproduced, distributed, or transmitted in any form or by any means, including photocopying, recording, or other electronic or mechanical methods, without the prior written permission of the publisher, except in the case of brief quotations embodied in critical reviews and certain other noncommercial uses permitted by copyright law.

First Printing, 2019.

ISBN: 978-1-951573-07-2

www.myskillsbooks.com

Good Morning! It's time to wake up and start the day.

First, I go and use the bathroom.

Then, I wash my hands.

Next, I wash my face with soap and water.

After I wash my face, I get a towel and dry my face.

I grab my toothbrush and toothpaste to brush my teeth.

Now that my teeth and face are clean, I get dressed in my new school clothes.

After I get dressed, I make my bed.

I pack my backpack with all the things I need for the school day.

It's almost time to go! I put on my favorite pair of shoes.

I see the school bus! It's time to go!
I leave the house and lock the door.

I walk onto the school bus.

I find my seat, now we are ready to go!
I can't wait to have a fun day at school!

Book Details

Story Word Count: 136

Key Words: School, Ready. Get, Bus, Wash, Backpack, Clothes, On

Comprehension Check

- What was the story about?
- Where is she going?
- What does she pack the thing's she needs in?

Reading Award

This certificate goes to:

_____

for reading "I Can Get Ready For School"

Good Job!

More books, apps and resources at myskillsbooks.com

www.ingramcontent.com/pod-product-compliance
Lightning Source LLC
Chambersburg PA
CBHW042111090526
44592CB00004B/82